Inside the NFL

Philadelphia Eagles

BY ZACH WYNER

AV² provides enriched content that supplements and complements this book. Weigl's AV² books strive to create inspired learning and engage young minds in a total learning experience.

Your AV² Media Enhanced books come alive with...

Audio
Listen to sections of the book read aloud.

Key Words
Study vocabulary, and complete a matching word activity.

Video
Watch informative video clips.

Quizzes
Test your knowledge.

Go to www.av2books.com, and enter this book's unique code.

BOOK CODE

Y 6 1 4 4 4 3

Embedded Weblinks
Gain additional information for research.

Slide Show
View images and captions, and prepare a presentation.

AV² by Weigl brings you media enhanced books that support active learning.

Try This!
Complete activities and hands-on experiments.

... and much, much more!

Published by AV² by Weigl
350 5th Avenue, 59th Floor
New York, NY 10118
Websites: www.av2books.com   www.weigl.com

Library of Congress Control Number: 2014930782

ISBN 978-1-4896-0874-1 (hardcover)
ISBN 978-1-4896-0876-5 (single-user eBook)
ISBN 978-1-4896-0877-2 (multi-user eBook)

Printed in the United States of America in Brainerd, Minnesota
3 4 5 6 7 8 9 0   20 19 18 17 16

032016
080316

Project Coordinator Aaron Carr
Art Director Terry Paulhus

Photo Credits
Every reasonable effort has been made to trace ownership and to obtain permission to reprint copyright material. The publishers would be pleased to have any errors or omissions brought to their attention so that they may be corrected in subsequent printings.

Weigl acknowledges Getty Images as its primary image supplier for this title.

Philadelphia Eagles

CONTENTS

Introduction

When the Philadelphia Eagles were formed in 1931, the United States was suffering through the Great Depression. Due to the country's economic struggles, the Eagles had a hard time building a fan base. The owners of the new National Football League (NFL) franchise chose the name "Eagles" to celebrate the American worker. Ordinary Pennsylvanians, however, did not pay much attention. Most of them were working hard just to put food on the table.

These days, the Philadelphia Eagles are living through a period that could be described as an time of certainty. It is a certainty that no matter what is happening in the country, loyal fans will follow their team.

Like a college team, the Eagles have a fight song. "Fly Eagles Fly" is blasted during home games before the team is introduced.

t is almost equally certain that the Eagles will be competitive. The Eagles have risen to the top of the National Football Conference (NFC) Eastern Division even times since 2001, including a trip to the **Super Bowl** in 2004.

LeSean McCoy is the current starting running back for the Eagles. He was drafted by Philadelphia in 2009.

Stadium Lincoln Financial Field

Division National Football Conference (NFC) East

Head coach Chip Kelly

Location Philadelphia, Pennsylvania

NFL championships 1948, 1949, 1960

Nicknames Bird, Blitz Inc., Gang Green, Birds of Prey

26
Playoff Appearances

3
NFL Championships

13
Division Championships

History

ALMOST THERE

The Eagles have reached the playoffs 20 TIMES in the Super Bowl era, but are still searching for their first Super Bowl ring.

Donovan McNabb played 173 regular season games during his NFL career that spanned 13 seasons.

The Philadelphia Eagles were formed in 1933 and struggled for the better part of a decade. In 1944, however, top draft pick Steve Van Buren helped transform the Eagles into a winning team. The team posted winning records in six straight seasons and back-to-back NFL Championships in 1948 and 1949. After a period of decline, the Eagles made a comeback in 1960. Buck Shaw coached a team led by veteran players Norm Van Brocklin and Chuck Bednarik to the NFL Championship Game. On a frigid day in Philadelphia, the Eagles shocked the football world by beating the Green Bay Packers. In doing so, they won their third title and handed Packers' coach Vince Lombardi the only **postseason** defeat of his career.

The Eagles surged back to the top of the league in 1980 behind coach Dick Vermeil and quarterback Ron Jaworski. In their third straight playoff appearance, they advanced to the 1980 NFC Championship Game and beat the Dallas Cowboys. Randall Cunningham and Reggie White then led the Eagles to five postseason appearances from 1985 to 1995. Even after this recent success, Eagles' fans were not used to the consistency displayed by the team in the 2000s. Behind coach Andy Reid, quarterback Donovan McNabb, and safety Brian Dawkins, the Eagles made four straight conference championship games. The team then won an NFC Championship in 2004.

⌐ Quarterback Randall Cunningham replaced fan favorite Ron Jaworski during the 1986 season.

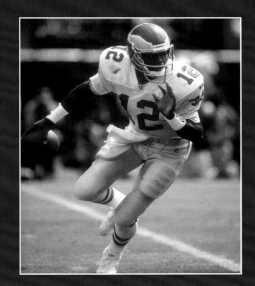

The Stadium

Lincoln Financial Field holds 68,532 cheering fans.

I n 2003, after 33 seasons at Philadelphia's Veterans Stadium, where the Eagles shared their home field with Major League Baseball's Philadelphia Phillies, the team moved into Lincoln Financial Field. While Veterans Stadium contained many fine memories, Eagles players and their opponents were eager to move on. Veterans Stadium's **artificial turf** was widely thought to be uneven with seams that caused numerous injuries.

According to separate studies in 1999 and 2006, the Eagles fans were the third most loyal group in the NFL.

Lincoln Financial Field has been a dramatic upgrade for players and fans. Named the NFL's "greenest" stadium, wind turbines and solar panels make up for 30 percent of the stadium's energy usage. Players appreciate its Desso GrassMaster playing surface, made of a combination of synthetic fibers and natural grass. In addition to hosting the Eagles, Lincoln Financial Field hosts rock concerts, soccer matches, college football, and men's lacrosse. In 2014, $125 million worth of renovations will create expanded seating, two new HD video boards, WiFi, and two connecting bridges for upper levels.

Hungry Eagles fans stop at Liberty Grill for a famous Philly cheesesteak sandwich, made with finely chopped and grilled steak, and smothered in cheese and onions.

Where They Play

CANADA

Washington

Oregon

Montana

North
Dakota

Minnesota

Lake
Superio

Idaho

South
Dakota

Wisconsin

Wyoming

Iowa

Illino

Nevada

Utah

Nebraska

California

Colorado

Kansas

Missouri

UNITED STATES

Arizona

New
Mexico

Oklahoma

Arkansas

Pacific
Ocean

Texas

Mis

Louisiana

Alaska

Hawai'i

MEXICO

Gulf of Mexico

0   500 Miles

0   500 km

0   100 Miles

0   100 km

AMERICAN FOOTBALL CONFERENCE

EAST		NORTH		SOUTH		WEST	
1	Gillette Stadium	5	FirstEnergy Stadium	9	EverBank Field	13	Arrowhead Stadium
2	MetLife Stadium	6	Heinz Field	10	LP Field	14	Sports Authority Field at Mile High
3	Ralph Wilson Stadium	7	M&T Bank Stadium	11	Lucas Oil Stadium	15	O.co Coliseum
4	Sun Life Stadium	8	Paul Brown Stadium	12	NRG Stadium	16	Qualcomm Stadium

Lincoln Financial Field

Location
1 Lincoln Financial Field Way
Philadelphia, Pennsylvania

Broke ground
May 7, 2001

Completed
August 3, 2003

Surface
Desso GrassMaster

Features
- two 27 by 96 foot (8.2 by 29.3 meter) HDTV scoreboards
- 172 executive suites
- 10,828 club seats
- two club lounges

LEGEND
- American Football Conference
- National Football Conference
- ★ Lincoln Financial Field

Map labels

Lake Michigan
Lake Huron
Lake Ontario
Lake Erie

New Hampshire
Vermont
Maine
New York
Massachusetts
Rhode Island
Connecticut
Pennsylvania
New Jersey
Delaware
Maryland
Ohio
West Virginia
Virginia
Kentucky
Tennessee
North Carolina
South Carolina
Georgia
Florida

Atlantic Ocean

0   250 Miles
0   250 Kilometers

NATIONAL FOOTBALL CONFERENCE

EAST	NORTH	SOUTH	WEST
17 AT&T Stadium	21 Ford Field	25 Bank of America Stadium	29 Levi's Stadium
18 FedExField	22 Lambeau Field	26 Georgia Dome	30 CenturyLink Field
19 Lincoln Financial Field	23 Mall of America Field	27 Mercedes-Benz Superdome	31 Edward Jones Dome
20 MetLife Stadium	24 Soldier Field	28 Raymond James Stadium	32 University of Phoenix Stadium

The Uniforms

TOO HOT!

The Eagles wear their white jerseys at home for preseason and daytime games in the first half of their schedule. When the weather gets colder, the team switches to their traditional green jerseys.

After replacing Michael Vick in week five of the 2013 season, Nick Foles completed 27 touchdown passes against 2 interceptions, leading the Eagles to a division title.

In their initial years, the Eagles wore the yellow and blue jerseys of the Frankford Yellow Jackets, a team that had ended in 1931 and whose uniforms were given to the Eagles. After experimenting with black and grey jerseys, green first appeared in 1943.

HOME

For many years, the Eagles wore a shade of green made popular by the Irish called "Kelly green," along with silver and white. An Eagle **logo** was added to the sleeve in 1989, and one year later, it was changed to an eagle's head.

AWAY

The 1996 jerseys were altered to "midnight green," a much darker shade than kelly green. In 2003, black shadows and silver trim were added to both white and green jerseys.

⌐ The bird pictured on the shoulder of Philadelphia's uniform is an American bald eagle.

The Helmets

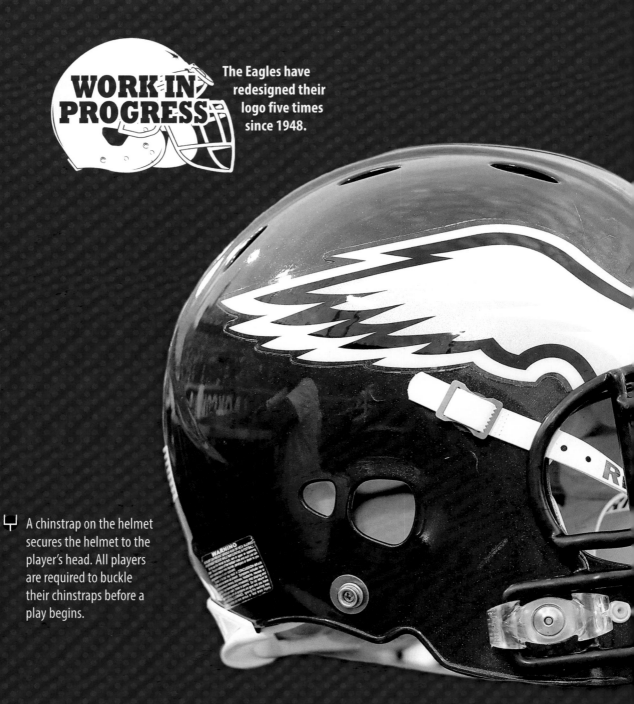

WORK IN PROGRESS

The Eagles have redesigned their logo five times since 1948.

A chinstrap on the helmet secures the helmet to the player's head. All players are required to buckle their chinstraps before a play begins.

I n the mid-1950s, the NFL changed their helmets from leather to plastic. The change was intended to protect players from terrible brain injuries. However, new helmets did not protect players from **concussions**. Soon after the change, team logos began appearing on the sides of the helmets.

In 1959, the Eagles changed from a solid green helmet to a Kelly green helmet with white wings on either side. Since then, very little about the helmet's design has changed. The colors of the helmet have changed from green, to white, and back to green. As this happened, the color of the wings changed from white, to green, and back to white. In 1980, the wings were changed to silver with a white outline. Since then, they have become increasingly detailed, with white, black, and silver giving the wings a sleeker appearance.

The Eagles are one of five NFL teams named after birds. The others are the Arizona Cardinals, Atlanta Falcons, Baltimore Ravens, and Seattle Seahawks.

The Coaches

5 Five different coaches have been named Coach of the Year while patrolling the Eagles' sideline, Alfred "Greasy" Neale, Buck Shaw, Dick Vermeil, Ray Rhodes, and Andy Reid.

Like his offense, Chip Kelly starts fast and won 10 games in his first season as the Eagles' head coach.

Coaching the Philadelphia Eagles may be the most stressful job in the NFL. In addition to having to manage bitter division rivalries, the head coach of the Eagles needs to manage the ire of the Philadelphia fans. While the Eagles' fans are amongst the most devoted in professional sports, they are also among the most critical.

DICK VERMEIL

Dick Vermeil won Coach of the Year awards for coaching high school, junior college, college, and professional football. When he came to Philadelphia in 1976, the Eagles had not made the **playoffs** in 15 years. From 1978 to 1981, Vermeil led the Eagles to four straight playoff appearances, and a trip to Super Bowl XV.

ANDY REID

In 14 seasons in Philadelphia, Andy Reid became the most successful Eagles' coach in team history, winning 130 regular-season games, six division titles, and a conference championship. Reid's Eagles came just short of bringing Philadelphia its first Super Bowl trophy, losing to the New England Patriots, 24-21, in Super Bowl XXXIX.

CHIP KELLY

In 2013, Chip Kelly took over for Any Reid. As the head coach at the University of Oregon, Kelly had taken the Ducks to national prominence with a **no huddle offense** that featured lots of quick passes and screen plays. In his first season in Philly, the Eagles were fourth in the NFL in scoring and won the NFC East.

The Mascot

⊔ Beyond being the mascot for the Philadelphia Eagles, Swoop is also the mascot name for five colleges, two community colleges, and a minor league baseball team.

Residing in Eagles Nest, a seating area high above Lincoln Financial Field, is the Eagles' mascot Swoop. Originally from Eagles Forest in Neshaminy State Park, Swoop is a 6-foot, 3-inch, 215-pound American bald eagle. Being a bird of prey, his diet is mostly made up of smaller birds such as Cardinals, Falcons, Ravens, and Seahawks. However, Swoop has been known to occasionally inhale a delicious cheesesteak.

In addition to entertaining Eagles fans at every home game, Swoop appears as an animated character on the weekly Eagles Kids Club television show. In fact, since 2005, Swoop has been the show's primary host. His television career has also extended to commercials, as Swoop has appeared in NFL Shop ads that appear during NFL games.

Swoop gained national fame when former Eagle wide receiver Terrell Owens impersonated his wing flapping to celebrate scoring a touchdown.

Sportslllustrated.com named Swoop the Mascot of the Year in 2007.

Legends of the Past

Many great players have suited up in the Eagles' green and black. A few of them have become icons of the team and the city it represents.

Reggie White

Position Defensive End
Seasons 15 (1985–2000)
Born December 19, 1961, in Chattanooga, Tennessee

Reggie White played the first eight of his 16 Pro Football **Hall of Fame** seasons with the Philadelphia Eagles. In that time, he set club records for **sacks** in a single season (21), and all-time sacks (124). When he retired, the two-time Defensive Player of the Year held a then-NFL record with 198.5 sacks. While the Eagles were not always great during White's stay, the way in which he dominated offenses ranks him as one of the greatest Eagles of all time. As an Eagle, White averaged more than one sack per game, and his 1.75 sacks per game in 1987 is an NFL record.

Donovan McNabb

A football and basketball star at Syracuse University, Donovan McNabb was well-known among sports fans at a young age. The last-place Eagles drafted McNabb with the second pick in the 1999 **NFL Draft.** No stranger to high expectations, McNabb thrived in Philadelphia, finding a way to enjoy every challenge football threw at him. McNabb led the Eagles to four straight NFC East division titles from 2001 to 2004, five NFC Championship Games, and a near victory in Super Bowl XXXIX. In the process, he became the Eagles' all-time leader in wins, pass completions, passing yards, and passing touchdowns.

Position Quarterback
Seasons 13 (1999–2011)
Born November 25, 1976, in Chicago, Illinois

Brian Dawkins

Known for his hawkish ball sense, Brian Dawkins patrolled the Eagles' defense for 13 seasons, making interceptions, timely hits, and blitzing for game changing sacks. His knack for the big play is demonstrated by his inclusion in the 20/20 Club, an exclusive group of 10 NFL players to amass 20 interceptions and 20 sacks in their careers. Dawkins was a leader in Philadelphia, the captain of a defense that went to four straight NFC Championship Games and reached a Super Bowl. During his time in an Eagles' uniform, he made seven **Pro Bowls** and was a four-time first-team **All-Pro**.

Position Safety
Seasons 16 (1996–2011)
Born October 13, 1973, in Jacksonville, Florida

Ron Jaworski

Nicknamed the "Polish Cannon" in high school, Ron Jaworski was also known as "Jaws" as a play on his name, and for his ferocity. He turned down an offer from Major League Baseball's St. Louis Cardinals to attend college. After beginning his pro football career in Los Angeles, Jaws came to Philadelphia in 1977, where head coach Dick Vermeil immediately named him starting quarterback. In a city that had suffered 16-straight seasons without seeing the playoffs, Jaws sparked a dramatic turnaround, leading the Eagles to four-straight playoff appearances. In 1980, Jaworski's finest year, he threw for 3,529 yards, 27 touchdowns, and led the Eagles over the Dallas Cowboys in the NFC Championship Game.

Position Quarterback
Seasons 15 (1974–1989)
Born March 23, 1951, in Lackawanna, New York

Stars of Today

Today's Eagles team is made up of many young, talented players who have proven that they are among the best players in the league.

LeSean McCoy

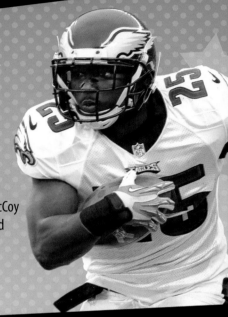

LeSean McCoy may be the most talented running back in the NFL. Combining blazing speed with great instincts and terrific hands, he is a dual threat out of the **backfield**, with the potential to take on defenses as a rusher or a receiver. Originally from Harrisburg, Pennsylvania, in 2011, this local legend turned Eagle star rushed for 1,309 yards and 17 touchdowns, and was named a first-team All-Pro. After a concussion limited his play in 2012, McCoy returned in excellent form. In 2013, he led the NFL in rushing yards (1,607) and **yards from scrimmage** (2,146).

Position Running Back
Seasons 5 (2009–2013)
Born July 12, 1988, in Harrisburg, Pennsylvania

Jeremy Maclin

As a freshman at the University of Missouri, Jeremy Maclin wasted no time establishing himself as a dangerous offensive weapon. He set the National Collegiate Athletic Association (NCAA) freshman record for yards from **scrimmage** with 2,776—an average of 198 yards per game. In his sophomore season, he collected 102 receptions and was named an All-American wide receiver. In 2010, Maclin had a breakout year for the Eagles, catching 70 passes for 964 yards and 10 touchdowns. In 2011 and 2012, he remained a primary receiving threat. In 2014, he looks to make a strong return from a knee injury that forced him to miss the entire 2013 season.

Position Wide Receiver
Seasons 4 (2009–2013)
Born May 11, 1988, in Chesterfield, Missouri

Nick Foles

Nick Foles was not supposed to be a starting quarterback in 2013. In the preseason, it was deemed that Michael Vick, the more mobile quarterback, would be better suited to run Chip Kelly's quick-passing, no-huddle offense. Michael Vick injured his hamstring and the rest is history.

In 2013, Nick Foles took the field and set an NFL record for touchdown to interception ratio with 27 touchdown passes to just two interceptions. In just 10 starts, Foles completed 64 percent of his passes for 2,891 yards and led all quarterbacks by posting a passer rating of 119.2, the third best in NFL history.

Position Quarterback
Seasons 2 (2012–2013)
Born January 20, 1989, in Austin, Texas

Trent Cole

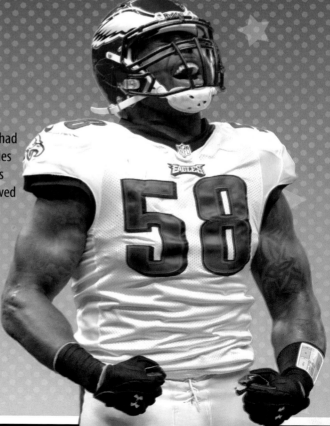

In Trent Cole's final season at the University of Cincinnati, he had 8.5 sacks and 22 tackles for a loss. Then, he came to the Eagles and put on 35 pounds. At 6-feet, 3-inches, and 270 pounds, Cole's extra muscle helped him match the level of domination he achieved in college.

In nine seasons with the Eagles, Cole has registered 79 sacks, placing him second in franchise history behind Reggie White. His size and speed give him great versatility, allowing him to play defensive end or outside linebacker. His knack for the big play was demonstrated by his team-high three forced fumbles in 2013.

Position Defensive End/Linebacker
Seasons 9 (2005–2013)
Born October 5, 1982, in Xenia, Ohio

All-Time Records

8,978
Career Receiving Yards

For 13 seasons, 6-foot, 8-inch tall wide receiver Harold Carmichael was a favorite target of Eagles quarterbacks. In 1973, Carmichael led the NFL in receptions (67) and receiving yards (1,116).

1,607
Single-season Rushing Yards

In 2013, LeSean McCoy broke Wilbert Montgomery's 34-year-old Eagles rushing record, gaining an average of 100.4 rushing yards per game.

130 Career Wins

With 130 regular-season wins, Andy Reid is the franchise's all-time leader. Reid's Eagles also won a franchise-record 19 playoff games.

32,873
Career Passing Yards

In 11 years as an Eagle, Donovan McNabb led the team to five NFC Championship Games and set a franchise record for passing yards.

124 Career Sacks

124 of Reggie White's 198.5 career sacks came as a Philadelphia Eagle. He led the NFL in sacks in back-to-back seasons in 1987 and 1988.

Timeline

Throughout the team's history, the Philadelphia Eagles have had many memorable events that have become defining moments for the team and its fans.

1943
With so many young men going off to fight in World War II, the 1943 Eagles do not have enough players to field a team. During the season, they combine with the Pittsburgh Steelers and are commonly referred to as the "Steagles."

1949
Behind the NFL's top offense and defense, the Eagles win a franchise-record 11 regular-season games and advance to the 1949 NFL Championship Game against the Los Angeles Rams. Steve Van Buren rushes for 196 yards on 31 carries, and the Eagles win their second straight NFL title, 14-0.

1930　**1940**　**1950**　**1960**　**1970**　**1980**

On December 19, 1948, the Eagles win their first NFL Championship.

1931
The Frankfurt Yellow Jackets go bankrupt and cease playing games. Later in the year, the NFL awards former University of Pennsylvania teammates Lud Wray and Bert Bell a franchise to take the Yellow Jackets' place. Two years later, the Philadelphia Eagles take the field for the first time.

1980
Jaworski throws for a career-best 3,529 yards and 27 touchdowns, while linebacker Bill Bergey and the Eagles' league-leading defense allow just 13.9 points per game. The Eagles beat the Dallas Cowboys in the NFC Championship to advance to their first Super Bowl. Unfortunately, the season ends in defeat, as they fall to the Oakland Raiders.

December 26, 1960
At Franklin Field, before a capacity crowd of 67,325 fans, and with temperatures as low as 21 °Fahrenheit (-6 °Celsius), the Philadelphia Eagles take a 17-13 fourth-quarter lead on a touchdown run by Ted Dean. Playing offense (center) and defense (linebacker), Chuck Bednarik makes the game's final tackle, and Eagles hold on to win their third NFL Championship.

1992
In Buddy Ryan's final season as head coach, the Eagles look tough all year. With 30 touchdown passes, Randall Cunningham has his best year in Philadelphia, and Reggie White and linebacker Seth Joyner lead a formidable defense. Despite high hopes, Philadelphia loses in the opening round of the playoffs to Washington.

The Future
With offensive talents like McCoy, Maclin, and Foles, Chip Kelly's up-tempo no huddle offense is sure to continue lighting up the scoreboard for years to come. The task will fall to veteran defenders DeMeco Ryans and Trent Cole to provide leadership for young standouts like Mychal Kendricks and Connor Barwin, develop a defensive identity, and try to keep their high-flying offense on the field as much as possible.

In Super Bowl XXIX, the Eagles fall to defending champion New England Patriots.

| 1990 | 1995 | 2000 | 2005 | 2010 | 2015 |

In 1999, the Eagles hire coach Andy Reid and draft quarterback Donovan McNabb.

1988
The Eagles win the NFC East for the first time since 1980 behind the play of Pro Bowlers Randall Cunningham, tight end Keith Jackson, and Reggie White, who once again leads the league in sacks, with 18. In the playoffs, the Eagles fall to the Chicago Bears, 20-12, in what would come to be known as the "Fog Bowl."

2013
After a pair of disappointing seasons, Andy Reid departs and Chip Kelly comes to Philadelphia. Michael Vick is hurt early in the season, opening the door for Nick Foles to have one of the best statistical seasons in quarterbacking history. LeSean McCoy leads the NFL in rushing and the Eagles return to the playoffs.

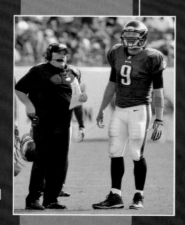

Write a Biography

Life Story

A person's life story can be the subject of a book. This kind of book is called a biography. Biographies often describe the lives of people who have achieved great success. These people may be alive today, or they may have lived many years ago. Reading a biography can help you learn more about a great person.

Get the Facts

Use this book, and research in the library and on the Internet, to find out more about your favorite Eagle. Learn as much about this player as you can. What position does he play? What are his statistics in important categories? Has he set any records? Also, be sure to write down key events in the person's life. What was his childhood like? What has he accomplished off the field? Is there anything else that makes this person special or unusual?

Use the Concept Web

A concept web is a useful research tool. Read the questions in the concept web on the following page. Answer the questions in your notebook. Your answers will help you write a biography.

Concept Web

☐

Adulthood
- Where does this individual currently reside?
- Does he or she have a family?

☐ **Your Opinion**
- What did you learn from the books you read in your research?
- Would you suggest these books to others?
- Was anything missing from these books?

☐ **Childhood**
- Where and when was this person born?
- Describe his or her parents, siblings, and friends.
- Did this person grow up in unusual circumstances?

☐

Accomplishments off the Field
- What is this person's life's work?
- Has he or she received awards or recognition for accomplishments?
- How have this person's accomplishments served others?

Write a Biography

☐

Help and Obstacles
- Did this individual have a positive attitude?
- Did he or she receive help from others?
- Did this person have a mentor?
- Did this person face any hardships?
- If so, how were the hardships overcome?

☐

Accomplishments on the Field
- What records does this person hold?
- What key games and plays have defined his or her career?
- What are his or her stats in categories important to his or her position?

☐ **Work and Preparation**
- What was this person's education?
- What was his or her work experience?
- How does this person work; what is the process he or she uses?

Trivia Time

Take this quiz to test your knowledge of the Philadelphia Eagles.
The answers are printed upside-down under each question.

1 How many NFL Championships have the Philadelphia Eagles won in their history?

A. Three

2 How many NFC Championship Games did the Eagles of the early 2000s play in a row?

A. Four

3 What quarterback led the Eagles to an NFC Championship in 1980?

A. Ron Jaworski

4 Who was the last Eagles running back to lead the NFL in rushing?

A. LeSean McCoy

5 Which Eagles coach won Coach of the Year awards for coaching high school, junior college, college, and professional football?

A. Dick Vermeil

6 Which Eagle set a franchise record with 21 sacks in 1987?

A. Reggie White

7 Which Eagles great played both offense and defense in the 1960 NFL Championship Game?

A. Chuck Bednarik

8 In 1943, what name did fans use when referring to the combined Pittsburgh Steelers/Philadelphia Eagles team?

A. Steagles

9 Which Eagles running back led his team to two straight NFL Championships in 1948 and 1949?

A. Steve Van Buren

10 Which NFL team went bankrupt in 1931, leading to the formation of the Eagles?

A. Frankfurt Yellow Jackets

Key Words

All-Pro: an NFL player judged to be the best in his position for a given season

artificial turf: any of various synthetic, carpetlike materials made to resemble turf and used as a playing surface for football and baseball fields

backfield: the area of play behind either the offensive or defensive line

concussions: state of temporary unconsciousness caused by a blow to the head

hall of fame: a group of persons judged to be outstanding, as in a sport or profession

logo: a symbol that stands for a team or organization

NFL Draft: an annual event where the NFL chooses college football players to be new team members

no huddle offense: an offensive style in which the offensive team avoids delays between plays

playoffs: the games played following the end of the regular season; six teams qualify: the four conference winners, and the two best teams that did not finish first in their conference, called wild cards

postseason: a sporting event that takes place after the end of the regular season

Pro Bowls: the annual all-star games for NFL players pitting the best players in the National Football Conference against the best players in the American Football Conference

sacks: a sack occurs when the quarterback is tackled behind the line of scrimmage before he can throw a forward pass

scrimmage: the yard-line on the field from which the play starts

Super Bowl: the NFL's annual championship game between the winning team from the NFC and the winning team from the AFC

yards from scrimmage: the total of rushing yards and receiving yards

Index

Log on to www.av2books.com

AV² by Weigl brings you media enhanced books that support active learning. Go to www.av2books.com, and enter the special code found on page 2 of this book. You will gain access to enriched and enhanced content that supplements and complements this book. Content includes video, audio, weblinks, quizzes, a slide show, and activities.

AV² Online Navigation

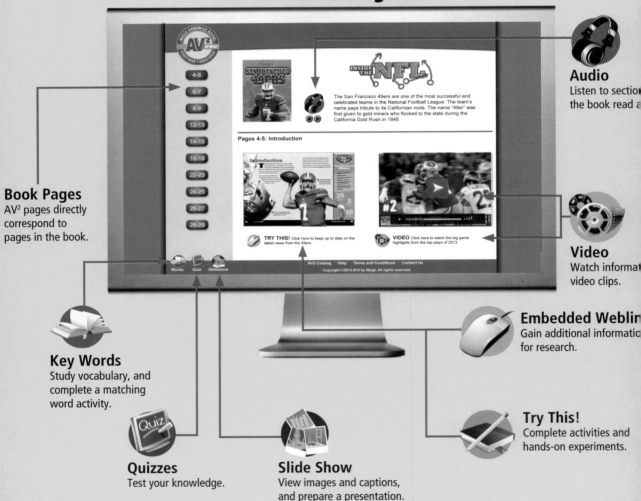

Book Pages
AV² pages directly correspond to pages in the book.

Audio
Listen to section the book read a

Video
Watch informat video clips.

Key Words
Study vocabulary, and complete a matching word activity.

Embedded Weblin
Gain additional informatio for research.

Quizzes
Test your knowledge.

Slide Show
View images and captions, and prepare a presentation.

Try This!
Complete activities and hands-on experiments.

AV² was built to bridge the gap between print and digital. We encourage you to tell us what you like and what you want to see in the future.

Sign up to be an AV² Ambassador at www.av2books.com/ambassador.

Due to the dynamic nature of the Internet, some of the URLs and activities provided as part of AV² by Weigl may have changed or ceased to exist. AV² by Weigl accepts no responsibility for any such changes. All media enhanced books are regularly monitored to update addresses and sites in a timely manner. Contact AV² by Weigl at 1-866-649-3445 or av2books@weigl.com with any questions, comments, or feedback.